HOW
THINGS
STACK
UP

michael castro

Cover art: section of *Blanket Country* by Michael Corr
Back cover photo of the author by Ros Crenshaw

ACKNOWLEDGEMENTS

The author extends thanks to the editors of the following
publications where some of these poems have previously appeared:
And What Rough Beast: Poems at the End of the Century; *The
Bloomsbury Anthology of Jewish American Poetry*; *Break Word
With the World*; *Bulletin of the Missouri Philological Society*;
Contact II Postcard Series; *Edge* (Japan); *First Harvest: Jewish
Writing in St. Louis (1991-1997)*; *Flood Stage: An Anthology of
Missouri Poets*; *Grist*; *Life, Liberty, and the Pursuit of Poetry*;
Light Year '86; *Literati Chicago*; *Long Shot*; *Memories & Memoirs:
Essays, Poems, Stories & Letters by Contemporary Missouri
Authors*; *Natural Bridge*; *Pathfinder*; *Pittsburgh Quarterly*; *Poems
for Your Pocket*; *Observable Readings 2006-2007*; *Sparks of Fire:
Blake in a New World Age*; *Shuffle Boil*; *The St. Louis Post-
Dispatch*; *Telephone*; *Untamed Ink*; *Winter Harvest: Jewish Writing
in St. Louis 2006-2011*; *World Edge* (Japan).

Published by Singing Bone Press
www.singingbonepress.com

ISBN 978-933439-03-0

for Adelia

TABLE OF CONTENTS

III *Patches of Light*

I. BLOW BIG MAN

BLOW BIG MAN

photo of David Hines blowing his horn:
belly & wrists protruding, as if bursting
out of his suit, right hand
holding trumpet, fingering valves,
mustached lips pursed, cheeks puffed, eyes
focused behind tinted shades,
left hand outstretched
leading the band

now in heaven
a spirit

Miles hangs on my wall
as well,
torn from a newspaper,
leaning back & leaning in

& Coltrane's up there too
as Roy DeCarava caught him
pouring light
They be blowing
their brains out
hovering over
my writing desk

We all just hanging here
in my basement
listening

Blow, they say,
silently,
blow Big Man,
blow

THE MAN WHO LOOKED INTO COLTRANE'S HORN

Me & my main man Mitch perched in the balcony
of the Village Theater waiting for Trane & sweating
that Summery May
be June of –was it '67?—I was almost
22 & anyway it was Trane's last year
in the flesh (if you can believe it)
the warm-up act?—Get this!—Ornette
& believe you me he had blown
us away. He had this Swedish bass player, David
Izenson (a balding descendent of the harpist king),
a modest man with a beat
would always surprise you & delight with his light
touch, & when he stroked with his bow you wanted to bow
before the otherworldly beauty, the fertile sound-shape,
you wanted to bury your head in the cave
of that Venus of Venusdorf resonating to his biblical embrace.
Right then I began a love affair
with the fat fat fiddle & we wondered
how anyone could follow such a set
had set the stage, warmed us up to fever fervor,
tuned our sensory apparatus to frequencies so fine
you could see
ghosts of the Yiddish theatre this dusty cavern used to be
floating by the drab curtain—Menasha Skulnick dapper, bobbing
to the b-b-boom, b-b-boom beat, the snake charming wail
of klezmer café reverie, & Molly Goldberg leaning out the window
of yenta heaven, shifting her spot lit palm from *oy vey*! mouth
to lotus ear, to shading sax-squinting eyes
as if peering down the tunnel of some lost subway
station of the cross-
eyed homeless goddess searching for the Trane who now was
officially late—late as only a ghost can know—no one
produced Yiddish plays anymore—the language was dying—
but the jazz of language,
the funny language of jazz still lived
at the Village Theatre & the Trane that we all came to catch,

& be borne away by,
that Trane was overdue.

Though the air had been conditioned to a degree,
it had not been cooled.
We were hot & damp in the dusty seats, drifting, leaning
back to where we were—New York, the Lower East Side,
the Sixties—
The mean streets leaned in,
hairy with hippies, skittish with speed freaks,
pulsing with poor Puerto Ricans.
                    Only the Village Theatre
& the well fed cockroaches remained
from storied days of threadbare immigrant memories.
Trane would come, Trane would take us away.
But who knew Trane himself
was dying? O sure, the sun, Ra,
was dying too. In time. But more
immediately . . .
Dying was Vietnam, Vietnam's
death consciousness
was everywhere.
Vietnam had our numbers & Mitch & I were going
anywhere but there—Canada, jail,
certifiably nuts—1-Y, 4-F, CO, AWOL, whatever
it took to avoid that cold, drafty death-trip.
JFK was long gone. LBJ had saddled up
the fat bullet bombs.
Bobby, Martin, Malcolm—their days were numbered too.
But Trane? Trane was like Bird, I mean
his notes were scribed in the air. In the cosmos. & now
we sensed he was in the hall. You could hear the shuffling
backstage. & suddenly, without fanfare, the curtain sidled open.

Dark forms crowded the shrouded stage.
We could make out Alice stomping
chords on the baby grand, & that must have been Jimmy
Garrison plucky at the bass,
& they were flanked by an assemblage

of street wise percussionists—congas, bongos, traps, gongs,
talking drums, bell trees, mbiras, dombeks, vibes—all emoting
a kind of cacophonous swelling, a biomorphic mass
vibrating something like thunder or bird thought shifting
to the sound they say a tornado makes up close
swirling over the hillside. The ensemble
built a kind of primordial chaos, something
from the nothingness they shared, that shared them,
taking away our breath, & restoring us
to a breathless awareness, an alert anticipation
of an electrical storm of violent renewal—

& then Trane emerged from the wings like a god
blowing in full stride & he reached out
with a finger of sound to the assembled host charging
the eye of their hurricanish brew with a gleam of life's coherent
insistent yearning, & they & we were off,
flying—Trane was down to earth,
businesslike in an unremarkable brown suit. His face was
serious & intense & he was blowing something beyond
harmony & rhythm, melodic snatches from riverbanks of memory,
from the silt of the soul, interspersed between cries,
moans & laughs, & another music that was as if
he had wired his brain for sound & was playing the 90%
we supposedly don't use, levels of consciousness finding form
& expression in the awesome moment, the world's
madnesses & wars
swallowed up in his inspired breath
& spit out with all their raw & jagged edges
painful & explosive & expansive—
horribly beautiful in the larger patterns.
There was a point—how far into the set I couldn't say—
but after the initial shamanic shock we were with him,
beyond musical or chronological time—
but a point in this newly created space was reached
when something strange
went down. A man rose from his aisle seat like an island
rising from the sea, a long, lanky, bald-headed, blue
pea-coated black man rose, & as if drawn by an invisible life-line

bounded over the sound waves & leapt onto the floating stage
to stand & shimmer & smile mesmerically close
to the saxophonic source.
Trane took no notice, immersed in his immense immanence,
& the man smilingly swayed as Coltrane played . . . a few of my
favorite things . . . *booh-waah! eeyaah!* . . .
       as Trane took us out
to those uncharted places once again the man shook
electrically registering each shock
wave & then turned
& peered down into the depths
of Trane's horn for forever it seemed
& then he looked back out at the oceanic
audience beatific & believing like Big Foot
must have appeared after he stared into the hat of the Ghost
Dance prophet & saw in that emptiness
the whole world—

Trane kept playing & the man stayed up there swaying
& then suddenly Trane stopped, nodded to Alice & let her lead
the percussive swells of the underlying sound-sea, & he turned
& threw his arm around the silent witness, & walked him toward
the wings, whispering god
knows what
in his ear. The man
clambered down the side stage steps & back to his seat on the aisle
& within moments Trane returned to make us gasp
with his rumbling
train of thought, & then again the man bounded & leaped aboard
& swayed & grimaced & smiled & buried his head deep
into the golden Selmer flume so that we could see the light
of spot gleaming off his bald brown dome as Trane played
implacably unperturbed through the intrusion, literally played
through the head
of the magnetized initiate—undampened, unwound
galactic, genetic spirals of philosophic sound—played
from some invisible mountaintop
through all our heads the unfamiliar familiar epic notes,
mapped journeys through this world & others

& brought us all home to

A Love Supreme
A Love Supreme
A Love Supreme

      *

eventually
      the man left the stage
      shaking his ringing head
eventually
      we all left the theatre
      to travel our own
      seedy East Village streets
eventually
      even the ghosts left
      the Village Theatre
      to its incarnation as the Fillmore East rock
      palace, & suddenly

Trane left the set,
left this plane & planet
whose pain & madness & beauty
      he'd exposed
to his obeah belly & breath—
having spit his medicinal music on us
through his healing horn & falseface lips,
      Trane left us one night
insights, lessons, sounds,
ringing his bottomless bell through all our heads,
like a blue locomotive Trane left us
& kept on playing

through, beyond

all the wars
& all the love
in eternity
within us all

IF YA WANNA RIDE IT
GOTTA RIDE IT LIKE YA FIND IT

Trust the flow Joe
   you never know
   just where you'll go
   but you get there o-
   k—here today
   as they say
   what?

   Trust the flow Joe
the juice'll rush
the river gush
& pause because
it must—
     The laws
the laws are in-
electable—
     the shadow
cannot be held
o no

   Trust the flow Joe
just try & meld
yourself into the fabric
of the whole—
not to say
in any way
     the soul—
but just the blend
of tree & roots & earth
     or
on another plane
the simultaneous birth
   of breath
   & death
remains

unexplained

Trust the flow Joe
whatever you did is done
whatever you had is gone
you'll never find
   what's left behind
yet today's new sun
   is the same old one
& the waves you've begun
   keep moving on

Trust the flow Joe

FOOL POEM # 1

for poets

Here we go with another
session
   pounding keys as if
to re-shape them to fit
   supple locks, & open
stubborn doors.
   O god!
the futility & the vanity
   of such an effort at dis-
covery!
   Tripping
over one's own shadow
   trying to pound
      even from sound
the stone's blood.
   Always the image
      of the Fool dances by,
some cuddly hellhound yapping
   at his heels,
               the canyon

   yawning

AUGUST 1982: MISSOURI
& America Lose Three Poets to Death

(for Tom McAfee, Mbembe Milton Smith,
& Arthur Brown)

3 MISSOURI POETS DEAD!

headlines don't read

A profound silence
aches the head
attacks the heart
of America—Columbia,
Kansas City, St. Louis—
highland, plain, & river
towns hoarse with grief,
flowers wilting in the heat,
hearses drift down sleepy downtown streets
voices gone downstream
unheard beneath the river murmur
of blood & bones, roots & earth

These dog-days leave us panting,
chanting ancient prayers, public
praise songs & private curses,
wiped out & weeping,
sweating & sleeping,
huddled together silent
& disbelieving, gently reaching
out hesitant fingers to touch
each other's still
live damp flesh

The death of a poet
is a terrible thing,
& three of our tribe have gone
these dog-days
answering cries of the lost

        guide Cerburus,
tuned to dark barks
we can't quite
              hear
draw
                near

O cities of the heart
enduring your dull, dumb pain
with dazed expression
News sheets cover your poets,
bury them on back pages,
noticing death in tiny type

Reporters who ignored
sit bored at "hearings" & don't attend
spirits' fluted whispers or saxophone shrieks—
More important stories
out there, they dream,
than the cool facts
of life & death laid out here

                OBITUARILY—

the poets' language,
spirit,
consciousness
that touched us

untouched

        the dream,
the press
of who we are,
were, can be
that Tom, Mbembe, Arthur released—

mappers of this territory:
highland, plain, & river—

       unaddressed,
       uncaressed,
       suppressed,
       depressed

    valleys of America
          yawned
as wispy McAfee smoked
in his wasting cancer
& spoke the intense spaces
between you & me;

& Mbembe opened the window
to let in light
of a clear mean broken bottle of a day
down on the corner
then leaped;

& Arthur scribed & sung his river
song & oceanic vision
then suddenly drowned in the flood
of a fluttering heart

Who would not sing for these who
themselves sang
deeply the bittersweet
poetics of life, the treasured curse
    of our space, our place, our
multi-uni-verse

Who would not sing, indeed
for the poets
       who sang for us
these dog days under the hot sun

We ache for our friends,
our vigorous & strong voices,
for the music unheard

on the radio,
the news not noted
    in the papers,
the images unresolved
    on the tv—

we ache for the void inside us

Three of our tribe are gone
these dog days
Three voices
        still

        in mind

THE LONELINESS & GENEROSITY OF THE WORD
for Robert Creeley (1926-2005)

painful
to watch,
hear,
in the 9 a.m. modern
poetry class,
you struggling
to find the right

word, right
phrase, *that is*,
you spoke,
haltingly, *i.e.*

in short bursts,
inhaled back,
& tried again,
two steps
forward, one . . .
like they say,
you'd say,

grimace,
narrow
yr good right eye,
as if to see more
clearly, *i mean*,
clearly enough to

satisfy

yr good ear

CHILI-MAC
for Allen Ginsberg (1926-1997)

Poets want Irv's Good Food
not because of the sight rhyme
but because this is a real diner,
white tiled exterior
& spinning counter stools—
the last of a dying breed
in South St. Louis.

Greasy menus,
Nehru capped cook,
lone gray waitress,
wino's & investment brokers—
all bow & nod
to its egalitarian fare.

A genuine place.
Bus stop pacers get invited in
out of the cold.
Everyone knows everyone—if you're new
you're soon known. No need
to introduce yourself.
Irv & his crew will name you.
                    Ginsberg
came in & tried the Chili-Mac Special,
grilled the cook
about how to make it,
for who, & why.
Is it popular? The interrogation
went on & on. Social
research.
It all boiled down
to three words.

Cheap and Filling.

Allen looked at me.

More for less, I said.
Like good poetry, he smiled.

We ordered some & it filled the bill.
More American than apple pie.
Yankee Doodle's Italian pasta,
the feather in his cap,
tickling Native American beans & peppers.
Multi-cultural dialogue afloat
in the gastric juices.
Irv asked, "Is it good?"

It was a good year
before I needed to go back.
Allen long gone
from Burroughs' home town.

I walked in the door & was greeted like a regular.
"Howyadoin' Bud?" said the chef.
"Well, well, well, Mr. Budget,"
chimed in the waitress.
"Where's Mac?" the chef asked.
I looked at him weird.
"You know,
your friend with the beard," he said.
"Chili-Mac."

POET IN A TREE
for Gabor G. Gyukics

prune it down
to focus the energy

don't be afraid
to go out on a limb

BLUES FOR THE MUSE

O Muse, thou givest me
the Blues
I ope my door to let you in
my empty room
& you send chilling breezes
in yr stead
that ache my knees
& shake my head
with images of gloom & doom

O Muse, thou givest me
the Blues
Yr absence takes my breath away
leaving nothing to inspire
My pen is for your hire
I offer you my golden soul
Yet you play hard to get
A wet
blanket for my smoldering fire
A shovel for my hole

O Muse, thou givest me
the Blues
The page weeps in white silence
The computer screen sobs all blank & blue
like my mind, left darkened by yr absence—
You do me violence, sad but true
without yr pacific, oceanic touch,
the waves of words don't flow
A constant ebbing marks me now
Limp, I need your crutch

O Muse, thou givest me
the Blues
But maybe I'll just take 'em
& make 'em mine

& etch a song to mark a stark dark time
of abandonment & not abandon
Then at least I'll keep my hand in
motion with emotion, stir up some dark potion
whose rank smell will twitch yr nose
with pangs of curiosity that say, don't blow, go
see—
& bring you back to me

O Muse, thou givest me
the Blues
& so I thank you with a curse
Blank Bitch, it could be worse
The Blues was good enough for Lightnin,
Leadbelly, Muddy, Blind Boy, & the rest
Maybe it's your flipside, Muse, your shiny head's
dull blurry tail,
your sunrise setting in the west—
Still lover of your light, I vow now not to fail,
but to wail, & accept your test.

*

O Muse, thou givest me the Blues

WARRIOR POET

I am Poet-General of the Army of Love.
My uniform is my human skin.
My shining medals are my eyes.
With concentrated effort
I deploy my forces:
Breath, Words, Poems.
We are prepared for Struggle.
We sail the Cosmic Sea.
We fly the sky of Vision.
We ride the curvy currents of Time & Space.
Alighting, we advance toward you:
Dancing to the beat of the Heart;
Shocking & awing with explosions of Spirit;
Breath propelling at lightning speed
Words precise & deadly,
Poems fueled by the Soul's nuclear power—
Invasive weapons of Mass Conjunction.

The super weapon: a still, small voice—
Penetrating your defenses.

Surrender your self!
Victory!

Ah!

WORD SWORD

```
                w
                o
                r
                d
w o r d s w o r d s w o r d s w o r d s w o r d s
                w
                o
                r
                d
```

II. HOW THINGS STACK UP

HOW THINGS STACK UP
for Chathan Vyas

I stack my American coins in neat piles
on the rickety table before me:
quarters the foundational bottom,
followed by nickels, pennies, dimes.
A mini-tower of mini-money.
I leave my room for the Indian world
where the rupee is the language
of commerce, not value.
Value is smiles, family, friends, all
by the grace of God.

A quick exchange with Chathan:
"I have seen people go
from Heaven to Hell in a second,"
he says. Then, "Forget 'if'!
Eliminate 'if' from your vocabulary . . ."
says, "You can't live
in the past or in the future.
Now's the only time. Tomorrow
it could all be dust . . ."
waving his hand,
"Enough of philosophy,"
& stalks off.

I go upstairs, sit down,
brush the table with my foot.
The tower of coins,
so painstakingly erected,
tumbles, & clatters to the ground
in all directions.

BASEBALL
for Danny Spell

holy
cow—he
dropped the pop-
up, me
first chance at
first base

i could've
died

spit

in yr glove
sd the ump
to the distraught
ten yearolder

& so (sigh)
i did & i
rubbed the bubbly saliva in
with my bare hand

baseball can teach you
(nothing
      but)
         patience

sipping cigarettes, grandmas
sewing moebius seams
round horse's hide

      hide

you'd like to but you can't
so squint in the face
the glaring err-

roar

swaying on the sultry
porch, a rocker
& a radio, breezy,
keeping track

2 & 2
becomes 3
& 2, something
gives

i marched down broadway
with the St. Jude's Comets
in the opening day parade,
circa
       1957, Dyckman Little League,
181st St to 207th,
Inwood Park—the Big Apple—
struck out then
hit a homer
off the flamethrowing lefty, Billy Guinon
of the Good Shepherd Shamrocks,
line drive down the line . . .
opposite field . . .
the crowd rising

     in my mind
touch 'em all
itchy flannel uniform i
    loved
     holy
         green stained knees
wearing
       number 37

the glory
that was Roma's

Pizza—the hurler
like some heroic warrior
embronzened at the center
of a vast sundrenched
arena

the batter waving
a menacing wand

the deliberate
motion
slow   as   summer

pissy beer
          flattening
                    in the sun

the minds

of all the players,
coaches, umps,
all the fans

poised together

the ball
                    all
the world

hard
          to make good contact with
consistently

30 percent success
considered excellent, not including
fouls, & other empty
strikes

a certain
       mostly silent music
           a rhythm

       the coaches' signs

the crack
       the thump
           the count

comments from the peanut gallery
       we're talking
facts
       & figures, relationships, statistics, history

          swings

          missed

               opportunities
dreams

wind-ups
& deliveries

connections,

moments
of truth,
when everything coheres

mind & matter
motion & emotion

stan the man &
nature

of reality

    in the floating

        world

slider
curveball
knuckler
screwball
duster

smoke

SHEKINA

She rose, a creature of light,
a lily, rising in her dewy bed, stretched
her body of light & 13 rays shot out,
13 rays of consciousness materialized in the void
between sleeping & waking,
she rose & wrapped herself in 13 petals,
a Lily of the West, rising in morning's eastern light
above the saloon, rose to dance in the warm wind
of barroom bluster below, a dance hall gal,
     a Lily, a flower among the thorns
     in the Wild West of Creation.

              *

O the rednecks & roughnecks & rubber necks
that clattered through the swinging doors!
How they whistled & stomped & brawled & bled
for beauty & booze.
How they cut the decks of destiny
with dung-flecked fingers & gun-greased hands
how they reached out to pluck every fruit & flower
wavering before them in the bloodshot smoky light.

O how Lily danced!
O how her 13 leaves, her 13 feathered fans, rose
& fell, revealing & concealing her loveliness &
luminous core. How she engulfed the mind & soul
as she tantalized, & eluded their grasp.
How her hair flamed red as fire,
how she flared off warmth & glow,
& could not be held in hands or arms or mind.

O Lily of the West. I conceive your memory.
I saw you dance on the sawdust stage
of the Golden Slipper.

I was among the rollicking mine-ers who lay bags
of treasure alongside the footlights,
who showered you with powdered gold.
O you were powerful & radiant.
I saw your eye-beam humble a heckler,
your darting glance make a groper grovel,
your flash of disdain straighten up a crook.

O Lily, Lily. O holy flower, wholly
out of reach. How you stripped each petal
& glided with amazing grace in the soft eye of spot,
how you teased us, bumping & grinding down
to your bare
essentials,

how when the 13th feather floated
into the gaping pit of the awed orchestra,
it revealed you

gone.
            Just traces
of your movements
etched in the light

that darkening morn.

DAN DE LION

you used to stand so straight
so bright & light just like the sun

now so soon yr stooped & pooped
all frail & gray

& gone
to seed

AUGURIES OF EXPERIENCE

When man aspired
down he fell
losing Eden
finding Hell

Earth became
a suffering place
a path to death
the human race

& death meant fear
& awe & doubt
God cast aspiring
angels out

of Heaven
where He lived alone
contemplating
what He'd done

Love still lived
amidst the strife
Man took Woman
for a wife

In time
they struggled to be free
to use the knowledge
from the tree

But knowledge proved
a clever cage
mankind rattled
mad with rage

God just frowned
& tipped the pole
darkness fell
on every soul

BITTER PENANCE

Eating the apple might have been a mistake.
We bit off more than we can chew.
I wish I could spit it out

in Your Face

but, unfortunately,
it's stuck in my craw.

SATORI IN BUDAPEST

On the plain of Pest,
as I entered
the Dohany Street Synogogue,
the second largest in the world,
they cautioned me,
Keep Your Hat On.

& in Buda,
up on Castle Hill,
in Mathias Church,
named after the first nation builder,
I was chided:
Take Your Hat Off.

Confused,
I went to my friend, Gabor,
for advice.
"It's the same God,
isn't it?" I moaned.
"What does He want?
"Who's lying?"

"Both,"
he said.

        *

Then he looked at me
& smiled &
I understood—

poets are pagans.

ESCAPE TO PARADISE
a ghazal sandwich for Ed Boccia, poet & painter (1921-2012)

I.

The exploding fish cigar's smoke is a bother—
Makes it feel like the party's over . . . *wondering what comes next.*

Saggy, weary, alone together—
Was I ever really your lover? . . . *wondering what comes next.*

O yes, you chased me in my youth,
When I was quite the mover . . . *wondering what comes next.*

Days of splendor, clear blue skies,
Hard now to recover . . . *wondering what comes next.*

The time of the serpent is at hand.
Its bite stings like a mother . . . *wondering what comes next.*

A walking fish, a crucifix,
The snake has shed his cover . . . *wondering what comes next.*

I'll leave my skin to all my kin
To fight over with one another . . . *wondering what comes next.*

Where do we go when the lights go low,
Can you tell me brother? . . . *wondering what comes next.*

I'm stranded on this sandy shore;
Is that you on the other? . . . *wondering what comes next.*

II.

Idly viewing the water
We know the nature of things—

Looking away, the mind spins.
The whirlpool world sucks me down.
Paradise a good cigar to savor
till the moment it explodes,
& I drown in a rain of ashes.
Life has caught me with my pants down.
Slither around me. If the asp bites, let it.
The serpent is always at hand.
The apple dangling.
The hanged man.

Why did we ever leave the sea?
Crucify me with the fishes.
An I for an eye. A me for a we.
Idly viewing the water . . .

Alone together, a private island.
Every I-land bounded by a boundless sea.
But our vision is limited.
We can't see beyond the horizon.
We can't even see our true selves clearly.
Breathing clouds the mirror.
Trapped in seedy bodies,
love explodes with flashes of light
we become.
We bask in it, fading—a comforting afterglow,
a sunset. Selfless eyes—

Idly viewing the water, we know the nature of things.

III.

I remember vowing, Paradise or Die!
You led me to your garden on the sly . . . *& we were lovers*

In a strange light time stood still,
The bee nuzzled the flower's petal cup & drank it dry . . .
                                        sated lovers

The bee taught the flower to buzz,
The flower taught the bee to sigh . . . *learning lovers*

Two became one, the world one too,
The shore & the sea, the sea & the sky . . . *transcendent lovers*

We dreamed paradise in moments outside time,
& were pelted by alarm clocks by and by . . . *awakened lovers*

Two little people in one big world,
Plummeting so low, after soaring so high . . . *deep diving lovers*

Paradise like a palmful of ocean,
flows through our fingers in the blink of an eye . . . *clinging lovers*

Your song's an escape to Paradise, Castro,
or maybe just a plaintive cry . . . *for all lovers*

THE TRANSPLANT

I am a fugitive of the Big Apple.
Left it in my youth.
Began a quest for Truth.
Left behind the babble
of its brazen, craven towers.
Emerged into a natural space
& forged the track of hours.

I am a fugitive of the Big Apple.
Saw the garden overgrown.
Saw my actions overblown.
Saw the brambles & the briars
out on Mad Ave. blot the sun.
Whistled in the subway wind
& watched my sentence run.

I am a fugitive of the Big Apple.
Singing the Jerusalemic Blues.
Eating what I choose.
Left behind my father, split man
hattan, shed the sea.
Snaking with the river, inward.
Planted my own tree.

MR. PRYSTOWSKI

Mr Prystowski
taught us Bible in Sunday School
at Beth Am, The People's Temple.
He was younger, more attractive
than the other (all male) teachers:
Mr Bernstein, sweat glistening over his lips,
broadcasting the indecipherable
Hebrew lessons with shifting eyes,
desperate for the attention of spitball rolling twelve
year olds—
yet he taught me, in his junior high gig,
first shakespeare, romeo & juliet, as you like it,
especially the all the world's the stage speech

 & half-bemused, half-disgusted Mr. Riisman,
solving the problem of getting through the hour
by making us write uncollected
unfinished essays—copy the text if you like—
as a way to pass the time.
He'd read the newspaper.

But Mr Prystowski held us wrapped in his delivery
challenged us with questions, seduced us
with his youth, his good looks—
overcame the barrier
of his nerdy first name, Seymour, going by
the ultra-cool Sy—Mr Prystowski
taught us the Book of Job,
explored the deal between God & Satan
to test a man's faith, to torture someone,
to make a good man suffer—
loss of wealth, loss of children,
a body burning with boils, Mr. Prystowski,
Sy, described each catastrophe—How could Job
not cry out in his misery? he demands.
How could he not descry his God?

Or when the three friends come & offer comfort
& advice—don't blame God they say—
how their words ring hollow, Mr. Prystowski says.
"I am guiltless, free of transgression," Job insists.
"I am innocent, without iniquity," Job protests
(too much for God).

But he's right. O Kafka! O Josef K! O Jews
rejecting & projecting guilt with every breath,
feeling sorry for ourselves
saddled with our raw deal
tough-love, uncommunicative Father! God
speaks to Job though, boasts really,
about His power, echoes
the arguments of Job's three friends
indignantly—question Me!—
(& then throws some suffering their way
because even they weren't sincere enough for Him).
You can't win. Josef K. lies on a slab in the quarry,
like Isaac, the knife passes over him.
Job, cowed by God's words,
intimidated, Mr. Prystowski says,
by a vision of His awesome power, pledges his love
in terror—
Overwhelmed, awed, scared, realizing
his own insignificance,
Job becomes the exemplary devotee once again,
& his health & wealth are restored. Yet

yet the question, Mr. Prystowski points out, lingers:
(What about Job's dead kids?).
Life is unfair.

> "One man dies in robust health
> All tranquil & untroubled;
> His pails are full of milk;
> Another dies embittered,
> Never having tasted happiness.
> They both lie in the dust

And are covered with worms."

Why do good people suffer
while bad ones prosper?
Where is justice?
Mr. Prystowski implores,

hands outstretched, face pained,
demands we consider
the questions, the answer. "The answer,"
he says, "is
there is no answer."

"The answer is there is no answer."

What a thing for a twelve year old to ponder.

How could there be no answer.
O Mr. Prystowski, say it isn't so!
But Mr. Prystowski repeats, shaking his head:
"The answer is there is no answer."

K. finds the air rarefied, stifling,
in the attics of The Law.

We leave class puzzled & disappointed
to be left

hanging
beneath the tree of knowledge.

The answer is there is no answer.

The only lesson I remember
from my Sunday School daze.

LA AMERICA
(for *Moise Gadol, 1874-1941, editor & publisher
of* La America, *the first Judeo-Spanish language
newspaper in the United States, 1910-1925)*

Warrior for truth,
armed only with pen,
press, & knowledge
that language is power
the powerless don't know
they possess. *La America*,
your organ, vital
beat of a community body
politic, split into clans—
Salonika, Rhodes, Monastir,
Constantinople, Kastoria, Adrianople,
     Janina, Corfu,
the Lower East Side, Harlem—*La America*
          feeds all branches, nurtures
common root, transplants
ancient strength of language tree
                    to immigrant
     sidewalks,
                    dreams.

          Moses
of the ghetto, tablets
in your pockets, your jobs
are countless, hours endless;
          poverty is
                    timeless.

In the beginning
was the Word, Moise, & in *La America*
you/we begin again. Touch
each new arrival, every
     neighborhood group. Watch
     your watch, pause, think, drink

coffee, eat okra at a cheap cafe;
    plot, scheme
how to pay the bills; write
            notes:
this lunch
is research, remember
to mention the need for better food
in these Turkish corner joints
in the next edition
        (if you can get it out).

Then off to the next meeting, the next
argument, battle. Abuse & ridicule
your thanks. Bulgarians talk funny
they say. No matter.
Sephardim (believe you/me)
        are clannish, proud
with good reason—write
        ignorance, provinciality
the enemy; write poverty (a state
                of mind), write
                    ego,
                selfishness, stages
overcome—stress—
    through Unity. *Unidad. La
        America,* your organ, plays this song's
            vital beat
                over & over & over:

    Unity is Power.
    Language is
        consciousness:

        the media
            the message.

        (Write
    on, Ghetto Moe.
    Don't mince

words.

Remind us
        of Babel. Demand
respect, reject
charity, speak out
offensively, x
        centrically—know God
is one, too; in exile,
too.)
                Dead

                in 1941,
Hitler stalking kin,
broke, half-nuts, buried
by your rival, who could not arrange
a grave site next to your wife's, or
even among our people.
Unity is Power. Is

anybody listening?
        reading?
                praying?

You are remembered, Moise,
by a few, with wry smiles,
as that original
                that
    loco-meshugge

who claimed Christobal Colon was

    one of us, hustling,
not knuckling under,
                        discovering
yet another home,
                unfolding

        La America

BAKSHEESH

Old lady beggar at the Shiva temple gate,
body an accordion of wrinkles,
mouth a toothless flap, making
moaning music—

bak
      sheesh,
bak
      sheesh,

sad solo song of the current Kali Yuga

thin palsied hand
atremble to her mantra's drone;
worn thin coins jangling
in an ancient iron cup

TYRANT:
Execution of Romania's Ceaucescu

I am dead.
I am full of holes.
I lie in my own blood.
I don't breathe.
I generate
death. Death
consumes me.
I lie among my lies.
My image, on
thousands of walls,
desecrated, torn down.

Who loved me?

So many volunteered
for the firing squad
Christmas day,
they held a raffle
& the winners joyously fired.
Flies graze on my wounds.
Soon I'll be dumped in a hole.
Unceremoniously.
To live among worms.

"No matter how much you feed them
the worms are always hungry,"

Elena said. But she was
speaking of the people.
And we laughed, and gave the orders.
Former, carefree times.

Elena's dead too. Beyond
reach. Soon
they'll plow us under.
Even now I see no light.

I can hear their cheers.
Different now,
more sincere.
My soul aches.
I can't rise.
I'm dead.

*

I'll haunt them

UNDERGROWTH
after the Shoah

Train tracks overgrown with wild grass.
Roads to death overgrown with life.
Insistent life asserts identity
pushily, through the earth, needing

no classification, no numeration, no objectifying.
Whitman saw the grass's meaning
as "there is no death"—
in absolute terms; & maybe
he's right, in absolute terms,
but here, by these tracks,
we deal with relatives.

Memory likes the grass to grow
likes the new to blur, & cover, & bury,
prefers the smell of dewy grass & spring's promises
to that of mass graves at the end of the line.

& so we survive, overgrowing, overgrown,
pushing forward life
& would, if we could, ignore
who we are
in a deep & rooted sense,
letting life's grassy fragrances
prevail.
But we can't quite forget.

The anguished ghosts are sometimes as insistent
as the grass covering the tracks, they can haunt
like mist over the field
around the places where they arrived,
places in Europe,
& in us.

The whispers of the ghosts are persistent, pushy,
they make us uncomfortable, for they are sounds of those
whose tongues were severed from the world,
whose names were denied,
whose souls & divinity
brutalized, unrecognized—
& they whisper horrors,
in a soundless language,
of what was done to them,
of what can be done to us too,
for we bear
their imprint,
their names,
their blood

We too
are pushy with life.

And these voices within us
whisper & warn,
if you really listen,
in the pride of your identity,
in the pride of your assumed victimhood,
they tell of what you can become
on either side
of the awful human equation.

Enough of that.
We don't want to hear it.

But dealing with absolute facts,
relatively,

there are almost no Jews left living
in Greece now, where once, vaguely within memory,
there were many.
Silent voices,
speaking ghostly Ladino,
swell with the wind,

from time to time,
in Salonika, Jannina, Corfu.
The temples are desolate, decaying,
awesomely silent,
scrawled & slurred with graffiti.

And the tracks that
the people—
men, women, children,
they *were* people,
humans—
rode away on,
packed like freight,
the tracks
are covered with wild grass
a dark wind whispers through.

The wind moves
pushily
through the high grass
of the graves of Europe.

SO LONG

fool, fool,
bent like a gnome
fool, fool,
writing the poem
fool, fool,
wants to go home

i been a fool too long too long
i been a fool too long

fool, fool,
mirror mutters
fool, fool,
student stutters
fool, fool,
lover sputters

i been a fool too long too long
i been a fool too long

fool, fool,
fool day & night
fool, fool's
gold shining bright
fool, fool,
an apple says bite

i been a fool too long too long
i been a fool too long

fool, fool,
cool & calm
fool, fool,
dreaming the bomb
fool, fool,
meaning no harm

i been a fool too long too long
i been a fool too long

fool, fool, a look in the eye
fool, fool, born to die
fool, fool, wondering why

i been a fool too long too long
i been a fool too long

HALLOWEEN

Today all the hungry ghosts
wail
all the world's sorry chains
creak
all its light leaks
into the dark
where hidden horror lurks

It's Halloween!
gargoyley guys
& shrewy witches—
the underside
is the scratch we itches

A parade, in masquerade,
of tiny boys & girls, wide open
bags & palms, stream through seedy suburbs'
leaf-mealed lawns

innocents
trickling trick-less

stifling yawns

gathering more & more
door to door
treats
from shadowed neighbors' smiles
sweets & coins
dispensed straight up or
with weird & twisted, hidden wiles—

cold cash &
bidden fruit they there-
fore dare not grasp or eat
without exploratory

pause

preferably
laboratory
analysis

Once home
they sift through eager fingers
offerings that they sought, & brought

mull possibilities—
laced treats & hot pennies
strained food for thought—

& later bodiless, near
nauseous, overwrought,
they wrestle in the bed

wispy demons of the mind

reflections of this bitter world of humankind
whose cool coins', glad hands' & twisted smiles'
impact instead
may burn, or sicken, or, finally

kill you dead

TRICK OR TREAT
for Ira Cohen (1935-2011)

Horny rabbit hidden under your Hasidic fedora
Bickering doves rustling in your beard
Wilting bouquets swelling the folds of your black cloak
Magician, Wizard of Tangiers, Sage of Kathmandu,
You were he ultimate poetry trickster

Majoun Coyote, Panama Red, Akashic Recorder,
Mylar Mirror Man, Hunter & Gatherer
of sparks amidst the shards—
Hendrix in the fun-house, masked poets,
a toothless man with a skull in his hand—

Every image you created,
every word you wrote, was the truth, you warned us,
surreal as it might be—the morning headlines
printed on cat fur, postcard *satoris*,
Paul Celan books under your Afghan hat
Outwitting the Labyrinth's security system forever—

You subverted capitalism with slight of hand
You snapped your fingers & tweaked the mind with pictures
You invited us to a Tokyo birdhouse to drink Tokay perhaps
to fly, or at least be tickled by the feathers—insisting on Paradise
Now.

& in the final act,
you're standing on the window ledge, wings clipped,
poems & other sacred objects—"your shit" they called it—
warehoused in a locker in New Jersey—
"My shit?????" "My Life!!!!!" you roared,
threatening to plunge—
Dragged down by bedbugs & hospitals & *samsara*.

Now you bathe in the sacred underground river beneath Hardwar,
You & the other Holy Men in the ultimate *Kumbh Mehla*
immersed in the goddess

 & yet,
You & Mr. Natural were spotted sitting on a bench
on a traffic island on the Upper West Side.
Your spirit is walking the page on feet of gold.
Your eye is laughing in photographs, the moving
still pictures of eternity you directed,
starring your many friends—

Sorceror of sneezes, conjuror of treats,
You performed the ultimate trick:
You're gone but still here in the Living Theater.

III. PATCHES OF LIGHT

DON CHERRY LIVE

Don Cherry chants in Sanskrit,
Chants Japanese, chants African tongues.
Don Cherry does finger *mudras,*
steeples, knots, turns hands
inside out to palms up,
infinite giving gesture, invites
"try it."
Don Cherry strums *duzongoni,*
the hunter's guitar,
& hums.
Don Cherry's voice
trills like a bird.
Don Cherry blows
his pocket trumpet.
Sits on floor & tinkles
on a tiny piano.
Don Cherry works out
a new mind mantra—AAAAH.
Don Cherry's lighter than air.
Don Cherry's got hollow cheeks.
Don Cherry smiles
& light pours from his eyes.
Don Cherry gives us a chant
& improvises over it.
Don Cherry gives us the clap—
"You clap on the one
& you give on the four."
We make music
chanting & keeping beat
with Don Cherry.
Don Cherry blows over
us, trumpet in one hand,
orchestrating with the other.
Don Cherry accepts a white rose
& a red one, & a woman's smile—
& starts chanting.
Don Cherry ends in mid phrase, saying
"Maybe we should all go out
& look at the moon."

JIM AIGOE'S SATORI

Cottonwood trees
Wind
Shhhhh

PATCH OF LIGHT

In town for Adam's wedding on a gray weekend.
Time to kill in Columbus, where there is no sun—
except in Hopper's painting
in the museum I walk to in the rain.

It's stare there or stare at factory rooftops & blank-eyed
office buildings out my hotel window. I stare
instead, timelessly it seems at Hopper's painting—
at the woman sitting up on her bed, hugging her knees,
her nightgown pulled up around her waist. She is

staring out her window,
blank eyed, alone.
Nothing to see
but factory rooftops across the way,
empty walls, empty windows,
the bare walls inside her room,
& whatever's inside her head,
or mine, as she looks out,
inside, at me.

In the dim gallery, I can hear the roar
of torrential rain outside, but
the room
in the painting
is bright, seeming to light up
the corner of the museum
with its bleak scene.

In the painting,
the naked wall behind
the near naked woman
in the barren room
is illuminated by a patch of sun.

The patch nearly covers the entire wall.
It mirrors the shadowy shape of a framed window,
a window that is so important
in this Hopper painting, itself a window
I look through.

I stare fully at
the woman's empty stare—
her timeless glaze
connecting with my own—
drinking in her light
as the rain beats relentlessly outside.

I wind up walking through a downpour
carrying her impressed image, sitting in that room,
on that sun-drenched bed,
inside me. Carry it to the edge of my bed.

It is spring, the wedding season has begun.

Back in the hotel room, with my wet clothes off,
I too am filled with naked desire.
Looking out the window at empty office buildings
& decrepit factories
as the spring rain keeps up its patter.
I sit still, half dressed, damp,
until my eyes lift like hopeful flowers,
& a patch of light can be discerned
breaking through the cloud gray sky.

FOR MUCIUS
who paints in red

you thrust your arm
into the mythical fire—
a show of strength
to cow an enemy

the red of the fire
burns from the inside out—
your extended arm,
forged like iron,
glows,
your fingers
burst into flame;
from the inside out,
life burns,
blue at the core,
bleeds onto the canvas,
a field of red
ripples,
flows like molten lava,
red of war, hunger, desire,
red's different tones,
martial, martian, menstrual,
Mucius, your red,
transforming red, the only color
burning inside,
insatiable, relentless,
Hungarian,
red
doused with paprika,
red—

suffering
of the light

BY THE DANUBE

for Attila Jozsef & Gabor G. Gyukics

meditation by the statue of Attilla Jozsef
on the banks of the Danube
at the northern end of Budapest's corso,
no identifying signs around because no need,
everyone recognizes the mustachioed poet
sitting on humble wooden steps,
leaned over, hands dangling over knees,
intensely surveying the passing flow,
his cloak tossed off beside him,
statue flaking & cracked,
this is how he appeared
when he wrote "By the Danube,"
before he dove under a train,
this is where he watched an orange peel float by,
where he saw past, present, & future
in the waves, where all Hungarians,
all humanity going back to the primordial cell
spoke through him, where he became
the Universal One,
& told everyone
to get it together—
"By the Danube"
Gabor & I, his translators,
sit at his feet—
the Danube flows by timelessly

CALCUTTA
(with Tagore looking down from the wall)

Power outage at
   the College Street Coffee House—
     conversation still charged

JAIPUR JUNCTION

Dressed like a princess
she cleans her baby's bottom.

All around her, men lay stuporous
on the station platform;
announcements blare from the loudspeaker
in staticky Rajastani;
people drift by
in saris, dhotis, bowlers & bangles—
a signal bell is ringing somewhere—

she ignores it all, focused, absorbed
between her baby's bum
in love's silent, solemn ceremony.

Husband kneeling by her side
dressed in white,
Heirophant to her Priestess,
pouring oblations of sacred water
over her fervent hand.

The water keeps flowing.
The golden urn he tips in his hand
seems bottomless.

She digs deeply
between baby's rump cheeks' crack.

The infant boy is serene,
his eyes dreamy.

The day is warm.
Smoke from a portable stove is rising.
Under the steady stream of water,
baby's brown liquid turds trickle & ooze
through her jeweled fingers
onto the tracks below.

OLD PHOTOS

My 79 year old mother sifts through old photos—
finds some from her trip to "the islands"
with her "friend," a "very nice man"—says
"These you wouldn't be interested in,"

gathers them together, gives me the others,
the piles from after she met my father—
Her eyes are misty;

something's reawakened in her,
the tender way she holds
those old photographs,
meaningful only to her

PISSING IN THE GUTTER
(a poem full of ugly words in praise of Beauty)

We would interrupt the game of "Johnny Fuck!"
to piss in the gutter. Watching the streams of urine
fountaining in beautiful arcs and washing the filth
gathered along the curb downhill toward the sewer.
Johnny Fuck was a simple game, a variation on tag
adapted to the four box wide sidewalk—
the two outer regions represented "shore,"
the two inner ones the "river"
territory of Johnny Fuck—players would chant
"Johnny Fuck! Johnny Fuck!
         may I cross your river?"
& "Fuck" would reply,
"not unless you wear the color ___!"
(& he'd name his pleasure, the price of permission).
Those who could show the designated hue
on their public outer
or private innerwear, could float across free,
those who didn't had to negotiate his patrol,
trying to elude JF's Loch Ness Monster tag.
If touched, you became "It."
The best part of the game was the profane chant,
the thrill of ritually uttering the forbidden,
power-charged language.
"Johnny Fuck! Johnny Fuck!" Sounding it still
gives me perverse pleasure:
Beseeching chant, ugly as sin,
I, too, proudly projected
to appease the Lord of the River.

And the forbidden act of pissing in the gutter
naturally accompanied this artless
pastime, relieving
its boring repetition, its unique tension,
with release. Toeing our concrete shoreline,
River of Fuck to our rear,

ocean of gutter before us,
our penises bared to the summer air,
the exhaust of blind sloopy traffic
on Seaman Avenue, touching ourselves
with the vision of a self-generated
beauty!—from all that
was designated dirty & ugly.

Bubbles bursting in the curbside stream.
Flowing downhill.

A yellow river for Johnny Fuck.

TARLOSAURUS AT P.S. 98

Michael Tarlow is talking about dinosaurs again.
He knows more about them than anyone
in the sixth grade.
Mr Kaufman calls him Tarlosaurus Rex,
or Rex for short.
Michael Tarlow & Milton Jupiter
are always getting into trouble.
They like to sit together & giggle & shout out wisecracks.
Mr. Kaufman separated them,
putting one in the first seat in the first row
& the other in the last seat in the last row.
Now they shout more than they used to whisper.
They are unstoppable.
Milton Jupiter is the best punchball player in the sixth grade.
He is the only boy with a girlfriend.
He is tall & handsome & tells everyone
Jupiter is the God of Thunder.
Sometimes the Catholic kids argue with him
& occasionally the Jews.
Each thinks there is no other god than theirs.
I'm willing to let him steal their thunder,
as Mr Kaufman says,
'cause I know Milton Jupiter can beat me up.
Michael Tarlow claims dinosaurs were smarter than human beings
& maybe he is right.
I have seen skeletons of dinosaurs at
The Museum of Natural History.
I believe they would beat Milton Jupiter up,
probably eat him up
if he tried anything with them.
I believe Michael Tarlow would like
to be a dinosaur
& sit anywhere he wants.

BYE BYE BEARD, SO LONG 'STASH
for Jomo

My face now naked as when I was born.
I peer into the mirror at this strange
Stranger—
have I uncovered myself?
I stare long, hard,
turn, turn back again—
who is that unmasked man?

Good gray poet gone,
head compressed, chin receded,
nose enlarged, an ordinary
guy—cut, shaved
by his own son
like poor dead Kronos—revealed, exposed
as less than what he seemed.
In this act, the son proclaims
his manhood.
Father shorn, bared
of bearded illusions
of potency, no longer
leading man in legend of his own mind, more like
extra—good-bye
gray hairs
bye-bye beard
so long 'stash—
no more long thoughtful tugs tender self-caressings.
Only stubble dots my barren facial field.
Younger seeming, older feeling
unrecognizable
on my way to true who
is that fellow
invisibility—ah
oh, ugh, words fail, trail
off, who, whom, hum . . .

Son looks at my blankness,
fleshed face he's never seen
since plopped on planet,
some eighteen years.
He's been agitating for this day
since manhood at thirteen, came at me
in a moment of weakness, armed with shears.

Now he's unimpressed.

"Hmph, Dad," he says,
"grow a goat."

FOR MORRIE CAMHI (1928-1999)

This is a poem for my cousin Morrie
who I didn't meet till I was 42,
yet who I felt I knew
my entire life.
The first thing we did upon meeting
(in California) was pitch pennies
because we both had grown up in New York
as streetwise kids
& this ritual made up for
all those years & all those miles
had kept us apart.

I loved Morrie like an older brother.
I loved his photography.
I loved the idea
of another artist in the family.
I loved how he insisted
on forming a relationship
with his subjects
before he'd photograph them,
how he could trick them
into being human
before the camera's
paralyzing eye.
He'd provoke a response,
push their buttons
before he'd push the camera's,
play stone dumb if he'd have to
to dissolve their stony stiffness.

I loved how we loved
good food together,
how his parties always had
such a fantastic cast of characters,
and always included
a magician & a fortune teller,

to remind us that magic & prophecy
were alive in the world.

& I loved his hugs,
our special family embraces
with Adelia & Lynn,
our huddle
where the only play we called
was play itself.
I loved this man
who embraced so many,
who used every trick in the book
of the streets—shock, shame,
laughter, sorrow—
to lead you
to yourself.

He taught living fully
to the death, & dying
with dignity & grace,
affirming life & love
to his final breath.

HORN OF PLENTY
   for Maurice Malik King (1943-1994)

1.

Malik lays on the hospital bed, unconscious,
hooked to machines monitoring every bodily function,
comatose, breathing heavily, responsive
only to pinpricks, not to words.
We talk to him. Maybe he hears.
We tell him those things we don't normally.
How much we love him. How he is us.
We remember his vitality, his joy in living,
the beautiful music of his soul & gleaming
saxophone & eyes.
I don't want to remember him this way,
bloated, near naked, splotched with sores. I remember
the way he said my name, the lift it always gave. Brother
Malik,
if I could lift you now
out of this limbo,
out of this bed, out of this room & its white gloom,
I would. I would lift you gently,
like the notes of a golden horn
blown by the purest of breaths.

*

2.

One of the songs we blew
that spoke especially to you
described climbing a mountain
in a blinding blizzard, seeking to see
the other side—
the unmapped territory—
you went there with your horn of plenty
each time you picked it up—
you're there now brother—

the other side of the mountain high
is unmapped territory

*

3.

What did you play?
"Time & Condition," you'd say,
shaking your head.
"Time & Condition . . ."
Your tone poem
blown fresh every set,
nourishing as bread
straight out of the oven—

How ya doin'?

"Cake's all Dough," you said.

*

GETTING IT TOGETHER

Here is my cock, a derbied gent,
   rising to the occasion
    of a lady in need.

Here is everything, love, seed
   I bury in the soil of your soul.

Here we rock together
      on waves we create creating us,
      waves in which we merge   emerge
      constantly changing, two and one.

 Here I am, naked before you,
   crying softly your name.

Here, my love, here
    the inseparable, unnamable, uncontainable,
      spilling up onto your shore,
          seeping down into your core

MENAGERIE
(poem with a first line from an anonymous
fifteenth century verse)

I have a gentle cock
Its song my lady knows
It finds her on her pillow
She murmurs as it crows

I have a pretty pussy
as black as deepest night
That bristles when I pet her wrong
& purrs when I pet her right

I have a shy & tiny snake
that when excited spits
My lady's fond touch draws it out
She loves to play with it

I have an eager beaver
toothless as a sage
who gnaws my log both day & night
takes kisses for a wage

The cock plays with the pussy
The beaver with the snake
My lady & I laugh & sigh
until our limbs do ache

LOVE POEM 83

I reached out & touched you
with a poem, unaware
in my glory, my heightened con-
dition, spotlit on stage,
When I finally came down
to pass as one
among the other mortals
you greeted me—hello, good-
bye, with a kiss, fleeting
on the lips.
It stayed with me
as you have, these years—
longer than I would have
thought possible.
Your kiss. Souls.
Touched. Touching.
A quick exchange
suddenly more.

& more.
I cannot shake you.
Wriggle as I will.
A fish unraveling
a line . . . a poem . . .
a kiss.
Lines
to tie a moment
into twin loops.
A bow.
          We weave through
one
      another—

& the knot
holds.

THE DAILY GRIND

Going to work day after day, waking up to morning rituals,
meditate,
feed the cats, make the coffee, clean the litter box, drink, think,
face the gray, hope for light—the article about the thirty-seven year
employee on the verge of retirement: Any memories stand out?
It all kind of blurs together—is this why we're here?—a few sharp
memories of joy or despair, all else a muddle . . .

Belly rumbling the warmth of morning coffee, wife asleep upstairs,
cats napping, I sing, softly depressing keys—
my mother would confront me
the same way my wife now does—draw me out of my silent shell
the way a blank page can—this is what love wants,
what the poem wants—
To draw us toward intimacy, open us, read us like a book
joining minds & souls—I never was a philosophical poet,
always more visceral than intellectual, more sensual than concrete.
More musical than most, shaping breath to evaporative spirit—

I want you, your lips, your breasts, your central fire.
Warm me, nourish me, caress me, enfold me—
The deeper I dive within, the more I long for release:
Expression

TAKES

A Master on vibes,
Karl Berger sd:
"There are no mistakes.
You follow
your mistakes."

*

Scolding Naropa poets,
Phil Whalen pounded his ample belly:
"It come from here, damn it!
Here! Here!"

*

Robert Ferguson
responding to my comment,
"I really like your love poems,"
smiled, & drawled,
"All I write is love poems."

*

Dahveed Nelson,
one of the Last Poets,
was laughing,
& when I asked him why
he just kept smiling
a kind of shit-eating grin,
& shrugged, & looked around, & sd,
"just the wonder of it all,
that's all"

THE LAST POETS
for Dahveed Nelson

Let poetry live
on the human voice!
Let it sing
to the beat of the drum!

We pick up
your staccato delivery
at the doorstep of the soul,
read deep
your spirit news.

Truth is old
yet ever new.
Revolutionary,
the wheel keeps turning.
The last
inevitably
become the first.

The first are singing
your lasting song.

EIGHTEEN TIMELESS MINUTES

that Ann happened to be scrambling by the crevasse
in the cliff at Pueblo Alto
on the day of the solstice

& that she happened to look in
through the slit in the cliff face
down through the earth

& that she happened to see the spiral petroglyph
that no other visitor or worker at the park
had up to then sighted,

& that she happened to glance in to the hidden room
at that precise time
during the quadrennial eighteen-minute period

when the dagger of sunlight
bisects the spiral form
etched on the flat stone slab far back in time

& that she was the only person in the world
who could have realized & processed that observed
                information
& obsessed on it & developed it & understood it

& shared it with everyone else in the world
to the degree that she did,
& that it seemed she had been called

by the light
for that purpose—
the light admitted

by the boulders & rocks
placed so casually as to appear
randomly natural

by Anasazi, they say,
maybe means "old ones"—
no one remembers

the penetrant light
intersecting precisely
the stone slab's spiral's center

solstice & equinox—
'sun dagger'
they called it

marking time's sacrifice
on the sunshaft calendar,
the mysterious spiral

etched on the hidden flat stone slab—
& those surface stones
placed above by "Chacoan Einsteins"

just so, to appear random,
casually admitting also
the shadow of the moon,

in its nineteen year cycle
round earth as it turns,
marking that journey

on the nineteen turns
of the spiral on the altar—
strange unchanging changes

on altar shaped like coiled snakes,
snail shells & galaxies,
speaking a language of shadow & light

quadrennial sunshafts
piercing, dividing
solstice & equinox

moon shadow creeping
over the labyrinth
turn to turn year after year

round & round moving
further & further in
toward the center of the spiral—

Ann noted it all & how
in the nineteenth year
when the moon was furthest from the earth,

its hemispheric shadow
bisected the spiral perfectly—
& then Ann noticed

at the solstices that year
with moon & sun
in extreme relation to earth

moon at its furthest, sun its nearest
in the womb-like cleft in the cliff
moonshadow & sundagger

met
& were one
for eighteen timeless minutes

on the stone altar
at the center
of the spiral bed

     *

all this recorded
on page & on film
by Ann herself

awed & mystified
at time's dance &
its sacrifice—

this ritual language
of earth & universe,
of love & light & mind

WORKS BY MICHAEL CASTRO

POETRY

Ripple (with Michael Corr, Alan Fleck, & Jay Zelenka), poems & woodcuts, Hard Times Press, 1970.

The Kokopilau Cycle, Blue Cloud Quarterly Press, 1975, long poem.

Ghost Highways & Other Homes, Cornerstone Press, 1976, poems.

Cracks, The Cauldron Press, 1977, poems.

(US), Ridgeway Press, 1991, poems.

River City Rhapsody, (with Eugene B. Redmond, Jane Bidleman, and Marcia Cann, *Drum Voices Revue* Special Edition--poem for the inauguration of Freeman Bosley Jr. as St. Louis's first African-American Mayor), 1993.

The Man Who Looked Into Coltrane's Horn, Caliban Press, 1997, long poem.

Human Rites, Neshui Press, 2000, poems.

The Bush Years, JK Publishing, 2010, poems.

The Guide: Maimonides' Journey, Shulamis Press, 2014, long poem.

PROSE

Interpreting the Indian: Twentieth Century Poets and the Native American, University of New Mexico Press, 1984; paperback edition, University of Oklahoma Press, 1991.

TRANSLATIONS (with Gabor G. Gyukics)

Swimming in the Ground: Contemporary Hungarian Poetry, Neshui Press, 2001.

Gypsy Drill: Poems of Attila Balogh, Hungarian edition, Neshui Press, 2005.

A Transparent Lion: Selected Poetry of Attila Jozsef, Green Integer Books, 2006.

Terrenum (The Place of Time), poetry and art by Adam Gall, Hungarian edition, Budapest, Eletrajz Kalliatasok Publications, 2010.

RECORDINGS

Scenes from the Gateway, with Exiles: Jay Zelenka and Gregory Mills (Esfoma Recordings, 1987).

Freedom Ring: with the Fred Tompkins Poetry & Music Ensemble: (tompkinsjazz.com 2001).

Curve Extended, with the Fred Tomkins Poetry & Music Ensemble (tompkinsjazz.com 2004).

Deep Mirror with Joe Catalano (Freedonia Music 2008).

Kokopilau with J.D. Parran (Freedonia Music 2008).

Needle of Light with James Marshall's Human Arts Ensemble (Freedonia Music, 2011).

ABOUT THE AUTHOR

Michael Castro, called "a legend in St. Louis poetry" by Charles Guenther in the *St. Louis Post Dispatch*, is a widely published poet and translator. *How Things Stack Up* is his fifteenth book. Castro is a founder of the literary organization and magazine *River Styx*, in continuous operation since 1975. He has spread the word of poetry off the page for decades, organizing readings and hosting three literary radio programs. He has read his poems on three continents, including many collaborative performances with musicians. His aural/oral work is recorded on six albums. Castro is the recipient of the Guardian Angel of St. Louis Poetry Award from River Styx and the Warrior Poet Award from Word in Motion, both for lifetime achievement.